LETTERS TO A YOUNG GENERATION

LETTERS TO A YOUNG GENERATION

EDITED BY

AMANDA WILSON

9:10 PUBLISHING

LETTERS TO A YOUNG GENERATION
A 9:10 Publishing Book 978 0 957 13674 8

This edition published in 2014.

9:10 Publishing Ltd is Registered in England & Wales
Company No. 07979071
www.910publishing.com

A CIP catalogue record for this book is available
from the British Library.

Printed and bound in Great Britain by Marston Book Services Ltd.
www.marston.co.uk

'Our deepest fear is not that we are inadequate. Our deepest fear is that we are powerful beyond measure. It is our light, not our darkness that most frightens us. We ask ourselves, Who am I to be brilliant, gorgeous, talented, fabulous? Actually, who are you not to be? You are a child of God. Your playing small does not serve the world. There is nothing enlightened about shrinking so that other people won't feel insecure around you. We are all meant to shine, as children do. We were born to make manifest the glory of God that is within us. It's not just in some of us; it's in everyone. And as we let our own light shine, we unconsciously give other people permission to do the same. As we are liberated from our own fear, our presence automatically liberates others.'

Marianne Williamson

A RETURN TO LOVE: REFLECTIONS ON THE PRINCIPLES OF
"A COURSE IN MIRACLES"

CONTENTS

In loving memory of Gus Allman

9TH OCTOBER 1993 — 19TH FEBRUARY 2014

FOREWORD

Being brought up in an urban city surrounded by the typical challenges that modern day young people face we can collectively say that growing up 'aint easy.'

Many people now know us as Rough Copy, but before Rough Copy we were and still are Kaz, Sterling and Joey, 3 young boys who have become young men. The men we become will be absolutely determined by the experiences and decisions we make both now and in the future and of course the ones we have already made in our past.

When we heard about this book, immediately we asked our Manager (Mr H) who is one of the contributors how we can be involved; he is not only our manager but also our friend and mentor. He works with us not in the traditional sense of business management but moreso as a listening and understanding ear; giving advice and guidance but ultimately leaving us in a position to make our own decisions; just the same as these letters to young people will do for their readers.

It's interesting for us; we have been performing together now for the last 7 years, first as a group called SOS (Sons of Soul) and now for the last 4 years as Rough Copy. It's been difficult, in fact it's been close to impossible to keep our dream alive and still survive as young men trying to find their way in life, but I guess the reality is that we had found between us a common bond that each of us believed in. We trust/ed each other explicitly. We challenged each other constantly, laughed together, cried together, shared good times and bad times together but at no stage ever looked at quitting as an option. Yes we got tired, yes we questioned whether we were doing the right thing but because of our 'brotherhood' and the support that was available from our loved ones, both friends and family we could not quit! Yes we had a good run on the 10th season of *X Factor*, being semi-finalist has changed our lives, but I'm glad to say hasn't changed us. Why? Because of those words of wisdom that were shared with us by people who had our best interest at heart long before any public praise ever occurred. I guess what we are saying is that when there's a chance to take guidance it's a wise man that accepts that. Yes, be you, have a character, stand for something, even sometimes when no one believes, but be careful not to confuse assertiveness with arrogance! They can look similar but the effect they have is totally different.

We are really looking forward to reading all of the letters in this book and hoping to take life lessons from them; maybe all of them won't suit our personalities but the beauty of there being so many is that there will be variation in the styles and what doesn't suit one of us will suit the other.

Finally, thank you to the men who have contributed to this book. Becoming busy men ourselves, we understand that the time you have taken out of your hectic schedules to help others must have been difficult but you did it any-ways. But the last words go to the young boys and young men like us who will read this book. Well done for making a good decision. We know it is just one of the many you have made and will continue to make in your futures.

Kaz, Sterling & Joey
ROUGH COPY

13 LETTERS

REVEREND
LES ISAAC

DEAR YOUNG MAN

Let me introduce myself. My name is Les and I was born in Antigua in the West Indies, a very small island with a population of 80,000 people.

When I was six years old I had a big shock. I had just eaten a big lunch with my grandmother, my two sisters and my brother on a sunny Sunday afternoon. Suddenly my grandmother announced that we should get ourselves ready to go to the airport! We were going to fly to England.

One day I was in a very hot country with lots of space to play, lots of friends in my village and my school and the next day I was in a very strange country. It was cold, I had no friends and, instead of living in a village, I was surrounded by the grey concrete of a city and pavements full of people. I didn't even have a chance to say goodbye to my friends at school, in the village or at my church.

I wished that I could run all the way back to Antigua. Everything around me was very strange. All the houses were very close to one another, and I struggled to get used to this new culture. For the first time in my young life, I discovered that I was black. I learned this when other children called me all sorts of names because of the colour of my skin.

Worse was to come. After us children had been in London for about a year, my father left my mother. I could not express the way I felt; I was so sad and angry. But I remember very clearly thinking and saying to myself, when I grow up, become an adult and get married, I would not want my children to experience what I experienced and to go through this pain, disappointment and anger.

4

I have now been living in England for the past 50 years and for 32 of those years I have been married to my wife. We have two children, and I am grateful that they are both now married.

In my childhood and my teens I found my life was full of challenges and difficulties: leaving the home that I loved, rejection at school by other children and my father leaving us. I rebelled a great deal when I was about 13 years old. I got into fights at school, I was arrested by the police and had to appear in court, and I joined a youth gang. My mother found it very hard to cope with my rebellious ways and anger.

I was brought up to go to church, but I found it very boring and I was glad when I stopped going. However, as a teenager my mind began to turn to religion and faith. I knew that I had to change my thinking and attitude. I realised that I didn't have to become a victim of my own circumstances.

Just as I was getting over my rebelliousness and anger, my mother died at the young age of 38. Again I found myself angry, in great emotional pain, drained and with a sense of hopelessness. Yet I remembered that my mother had expectations for me. Deep down I knew that it was not what life threw at me that was the big thing but how I responded to it.

As I look back over the years of my life I have developed a strong sense that in spite of all my challenges, difficulties and disappointments, I could be someone who overcomes. I could be a positive role model for other people. In February 2013, I received the Order of the British Empire (OBE) from Her Majesty the Queen for my work across the United Kingdom.

It is not where you are coming from that really matters; it is where you are going in life. It is not how you start in life it is how you finish.

BLESSINGS,
Reverend Les Isaac

JULIAN E. GOLDING

DEAR YOUNG MAN,

My name is Julian E. Golding and I write this letter firstly to remind you that there is greatness within you and secondly to let you know that if you have a goal that you want to accomplish, it can come to fruition. Before you fulfill your goal, you have a responsibility to actively pursue that goal until it has been accomplished, regardless of the obstacles that may hinder you. Perseverance is a fundamental prerequisite for success, regardless of your background or socioeconomic status. If you really want something bad enough, you'll work hard enough to achieve it. I hope this letter helps to inspire you, to know with hard work and dedication, dreams can come true.

Now that I've got the preamble out of the way, I want to share my story of success along with the obligatory ups and downs, which makes any story of success more meaningful and worthwhile.

When I was nine years old, I remember watching the 1984 Los Angeles Olympic Games on an old black and white television (yes black and white!). An American sprinter named Carl Lewis was hot favourite to win four gold medals at a single Olympic Games. Lewis was the favourite to win the 100m, 200m, long jump and the 4x100m relay. If he managed to achieve this superhuman feat, he would have emulated the legendary Jesse Owens, who won four gold medals in exactly the same events, at the 1936 Berlin Olympic Games. Suffice to say, Lewis did win all four gold medals and is widely considered as one of the greatest Olympic athletes of all-time. His success at the 1984 Olympic Games was a display of poetry in motion, and he subsequently went on to win five more gold medals at three other Olympic Games, completely dominating the field of athletics. The name 'Carl Lewis' on the starting lists at any major athletics event rendered his opponents with fear and dread. Carl Lewis' equivalent today would be the Jamaican sprinter Usain Bolt, who has already equalled Carl Lewis' impressive medal haul.

So, you may be wondering, 'What's the big deal about Carl Lewis?' Well, he was my sporting role model growing up, and I remember vividly saying to myself, 'I would love to run for my country at a major athletics event and win lots of gold medals.' And guess what? . . . *I DID!*

During my secondary school days, I didn't take school seriously. By all accounts, I wasn't a bad student, sometimes a bit naughty and mildly disruptive but I always respected my teachers and knew how far to go. My biggest problem was that I was lazy and didn't recognise the importance of education and how it could have a major impact on my life as an adult. I believe school provides the building blocks for success and is the foundation for your future.

I come from a large family, and I'm the oldest of 5

siblings. I was brought up in a loving family environment with both parents. However, being the oldest child, I felt I was overlooked as far as my educational wellbeing was concerned.

My parents didn't really push me and as long as I wasn't getting into trouble they were fine. I wish I'd had a mentor, someone to show an interest in what I was doing and to investigate areas of my development. I don't blame my parents, because they did the best they could based on their own upbringing and knowledge. However I subsequently left school with only a GCSE grade C in English to my name! Five years of studying (or in my case not studying!) and only one GCSE. So, you might ask, where did I go from here?

I started athletics after I left school and some might have said that it was a bit late to be taking up a new sport at 16. But I never forgot the feelings I had as a young impressionable boy watching Carl Lewis all those years ago . . . my journey had now begun. My coach, Mike McFarlane, was a former international sprinter who I'd watched competing as a child. One day he approached me and said,

"I think you're talented and you've got a lot of potential . . . I think you should let me coach you, two days a week at the track". For the first time in my existence, somebody saw something that was intrinsically unique about me. Somebody wanted to invest their time, knowledge and experience in me so that I could achieve something in life. But little did I know how hard it was going to be.

There is a well-known saying, 'No pain, No gain!' I can honestly say, that if you really want to achieve something you have to work at it. It doesn't matter how talented you are, or how much money you may or may not have, you can't buy hard-work. I trained 2-3 days per week, I didn't go out partying with my friends or chasing girls, I had something I wanted to achieve and I didn't want to let anything distract me from achieving my objective.

I even had to be radical and sever links with some of my former friends. If you have friends that you know do not share the same value system as you or get involved in anti-social behaviour, those are not the friends you should be associated with. Unfortunately, those friends could potentially hinder you from achieving your goals. There is a well-known saying, 'Show me your friends, and I'll tell you who you are.' You can tell a lot about a person by the company they keep, and unfortunately I have friends that are no longer alive today because of the company they kept.

Within the first couple of years of training with my coach, I soon realised that he was the right person to coach me. He was firm but fair and he believed in me. I became the National Junior Champion at both the 100m and 200m respectfully and represented Great Britain at the World Junior Championships in Portugal. I progressed to the 100m finals finishing last, and won a gold medal as part of the 4x100m relay team. This bitter sweet experience at competing at this level made me realise that if I wanted to become a professional athlete my whole approach and attitude had to change. Due to my unexpected success as a junior athlete, I was quickly signed up to a major sports clothing company that paid me to a wear their clothes! Wow, I thought to myself, this boy from humble beginnings has arrived, but despite my lack of experience I became acutely aware that with success comes pressure and responsibility. I was now good enough to be paid for what I enjoyed doing,

12

running as fast as possible! I quickly progressed through the ranks winning various competitions and making a name for myself. I soon became recognised as one of Britain's up and coming talented sprinters and soon took up the mantle left by our 1992 Olympic 100m Champion Linford Christie.

At the 1998 European Athletics Championships in Budapest, I was the favourite to win the gold medal in the 200m. After running a series of fast times and winning both heats and semi-finals convincingly, I was en route to win my first major senior title. In the 200m final however, I was beaten by my team mate, and took home the bronze medal instead. Being beaten was an earth shattering experience. I went back to my hotel room, laid on the bed and cried like a baby. When I thought about all the days spent training, sacrifices I made and future plans, it all came down to this single moment and I'd failed. I then began to think about some of the great athletes like Carl Lewis. Against insurmountable pressure they seemed to perform at their best, so what was wrong with me? My coach began to reassure me that the guys that had beaten me, were not better than me, but rather I just ran a poor race on the day - just a bad day at the office. I told myself that the next opportunity I had to compete at a major championship I would not make the same mistake again, but simply put into practice what I did every day and run my own race. I had no control over the external influences such as the crowd, weather, TV cameras or my opponents, only on what I did.

The opportunity to perform again soon presented itself. In the same year, at the Kuala Lumpur Commonwealth Games, I was again the favourite to win. As a TV commentator described, I 'floated' to a personal best time of 20.34 seconds in the 200m semi-finals. I cannot begin to describe the anxiety I felt before the 200m final. All of my past poor races and insecurities were all magnified and the pressure to win was immense. But I reminded myself, 'Julian all you can do is run your own race and focus on your lane.' Everything else was out of my control, and with that said I went on to win the race and take home my first gold medal and my first major title - no one can ever take that away from me. In the 4 x 100m relay, I helped the England team win their second gold medal, setting a championship best performance time of 38.20 seconds, a Commonwealth Games record that still stands today.

One overwhelming memory from that competition was HRH Queen Elizabeth II presenting me with my gold medal; I never thought in a million years I would ever rub shoulders with royalty. As result of winning this gold medal I still continue to generate income from motivational talks and meet famous people in the process. I have subsequently been invited to Buckingham Palace on several occasions and have met with Prince Charles, having worked as a sporting ambassador for The Prince's Trust.

Young man, you'll never know what life brings, who you'll meet or where you'll travel. Your talent may take you across the globe, as I have, or allow you to rub shoulders with royalty. But one thing I will say, is to be the best you can be, and don't settle for second best. With hard-work, dedication, sacrifice and a love for what you enjoy, the sky is the limit. So, remove procrastination, fear, doubt, lack of confidence or low self-esteem as there is greatness within you waiting to burst out.

ALL THE BEST,

Julian E. Golding

JACOB
WHITTINGHAM

DEAR SIR,

   I bet you didn't know that if you leave school with no qualifications, you're likely to earn £6.93 per hour . . . if General Certificates of Secondary Education (GCSEs) are your highest qualifications, you're likely to earn £8.68 per hour . . . if your highest qualifications are A-Levels it's £10 per hour . . . and check this, with a degree on average you're likely to earn £16.10 per hour.

   That means that if you got a degree, you're likely to

earn 85% more than a guy with GCSEs as their highest qualification.

Nope, I didn't make them up, and yep, they're real. Forget what you hear about 'people with degrees not being able to find jobs' - these are the real stats, straight from the government's figures.

That's right, I put that at the beginning cos I wanted to get your attention. Cos if I said to you, ok so this letter's about how important it is to get a University degree, be honest ... you might've skipped to the next chapter, perhaps gone back onto FIFA, or checked your Insta. Just so you know, I don't take that kinda stuff personal ... I prob woulda done the same thing too ...

You see, the problem is this...right now young black men are more likely to be unemployed than any other ethnic group in the UK, with over one in four currently out of work. Yea it's peak. And part of that is because of the qualifications that many of these young men lack.

But you might be thinking, 'Bruv what about Richard Branson, I swear he left school aged 16 and that Don's worth over $4.6billion.'

And I'd say, 'Yeah but what they don't tell you about Richard Branson is that his dad was a well-off barrister, his grandfather was a High Court Judge, and before dropping out, he went to two very exclusive private schools. So he was always up.'

Then you'd say, 'Fam what about Bill Gates? That guy didn't even finish Uni' . . . and I'd reply . . . 'Yea, er Bill Gates was at Harvard at the time . . . plus his Dad was a prominent Lawyer, and his mum worked in Banking - so that guy could afford to leave his studies cos he always had back up . . .'

Plus what you'd be forgetting is that both these guy are white and wealthy. You're black and prob don't have the huge cash flow that they had at that time. So all I'm saying is, if you wanna get a JOB and get rich, you got two options:

Get the most powerful bleaching cream known to mankind . . . or get a degree.

But I know that you might still be holding out on me, saying, 'Wait, hold up, I don't necessarily need a degree to earn gwop - I can do that by kicking ball, or becoming a musician. Wretch and Sterling made it - so can I . . .'

The problem is that what certain people (we both know

who they are) don't wanna tell you is that 90% of music artists earn less than £15,000 a year, and 90% of songwriters/producers and composers earn less than £5,000 a year. Not good huh? Hey, I'm not saying you're not gonna be the next breakthrough artist, all I'm saying is that that's the long way round to earning cash . . . and getting the degree might sound boring, but it's the smart, logical and simple way to be up.

Oh and with kicking ball . . . hmmm . . . ok we all know that the average wage of a premiership footballer is around £409k per year, what a lot of people don't know is that most footballers will only get to a semi pro-level which pays around £25k per year. Not what you expected eh? You're probably thinking, 'but if I do 'make it' I can make more money in sport and music than I ever could in anything else so it's worth the gamble right?' Wrong! The richest people in the world are typically in business or finance, not in music or sport. In the Sunday Times UK Top 1000 Rich List 2012, under 30 were from the music industry, and around ten were from Sports. In other words, sports and music pays hardly anything compared to other professions

. . . professions that more often than not need a University degree.

Hey if you don't believe me - do the research. I'm just basing what I'm saying on cold, hard facts - not by the Rolex that Skepta wears.

Now I know you got it hard in school . . . trust me I been there . . . certain teachers get scared when you play fight thinking that it's something serious and want to exclude you . . . certain teachers calling security when you argue with the teachers cos they think you're being overly aggressive . . .

And we both know that's cos some (not all) of your teachers are pretty dumb - that means that they can't see beyond the BS they get fed on the TV . . . They watch Top Boy and they think you're all one step away from prison . . . they catch a glimpse of the stabbing in Peckham on the news and they think you're the kinda guy who'd shank them if you see them outta class . . . and when they briefly catch the MTV VMA awards they think you all wanna be Rick Ross, so they have low expectations for you. In short, it's hard for you because some teachers have already written

20

you off - and so don't wanna give you the attention you need to inspire you to wanna get that degree.

Whenever you feel that pressure from a teacher, just remember this brief story: You might know that there's a chain of pubs called JD Wetherspoon . . . you have them in town centres and stuff. Anyway, there was this guy called Tim Martin who was in school in the 1970s . . . and he had a teacher who always told him that he wouldn't amount to anything. This annoyed Tim Martin, so when he finished school, got his qualifications, and set up his first business, he decided to name it after his teacher . . . and he did that so that every time Mr Wetherspoon sees his name on that pub (all 880) he has to feel stupid . . . cos that company racked in £44.6million last year

This is kinda my way of saying that living well is the best revenge. Not getting yourself excluded. And not thinking that getting qualifications is a joke.

Cos bottom line is: you've always been smart. Nah scratch that, you've always been smartER. I could go on and on and tell you how the Dogon people in the African nation of Mali managed to develop technology to determine the precise position of star system Sirius that could not be seen from the naked eye . . . I could tell you amazing stories about how African-American slaves such as Frederick Douglass taught himself how to read . . . (imagine that!! The brother taught himself how to read!!) . . . I could speak for aaaages about how the Nigerian computer specialist, Philip Emeagwali helped develop the early technology behind the Internet back in the 1980s . . . (and that's aside from the Pyramids) . . .

. . . but I'd be saying all that because a) Black people have always been doing amazing things academically (we can do more than dance and spit bars y'know)! And b) because slyly, there's a reason why not many of us know about these achievements . . . and that's cos when you hear these things, you might get inspired, and when you get inspired in school, you excel, and when you excel, employers can't try to deny you that job . . . and that's disastrous for certain types of people . . .

You see I've got a sneaky suspicion that certain people wanna push all black males into kicking ball and spitting on tracks . . . cos while we all spend our time trying (and generally failing) to get a number one track or play for Arsenal, our only option is to get a job working as a security guard at TopShop - not that that's the end of the world - but what it does mean is that it leaves all the better paid jobs (stockbroking, lawyering, doctoring etc.) to the . . . ahem . . . other people.

So maybe, just maybe it's time we stopped giving everyone else the good jobs, and got that degree, so you can make that dough for you. And speaking personally, that's why I went and got a degree, and then a Masters, and then a Post Graduate Certificate (PGC) and a finally a Ph.D (yea that's right, I went and made sure I became a doctor) - so that now when I go for a job interview, no-one can say I'm not qualified for that position, and furthermore . . . I can tell them how much I should be paid - not the other way round.

A Jamaican Black activist called Marcus Garvey once wrote, 'a mind is a terrible thing to waste' . . . I would add, 'a mind is a terrible thing to waste because you've just wasted the chance to earn £200,000 over a lifetime more than those who don't have a degree.'

But hey, I don't wanna tell you what to do . . . you might

23

not wanna earn money . . . all I'm saying is that I kinda get
the feeling that you don't wanna be old, cold and poor in the
UK . . . Good luck brother whatever you decide . . .

#HardWorkIsLightWork

Jacob Whittingham

HUGH
QUARSHIE

DEAR JUNIOR,

When I was about your age, I didn't really think that my parents had much of a clue about what was going on. They seemed to be applying old rules and attitudes to a modern world, quite different to the one in which they had grown up. You must understand that my parents came to Britain shortly after Ghana became independent in 1957. They were proud to be African but yet had a high regard for the values and tastes of the old colonial master, Britain. They believed in

God and went to church. And I'm guessing they prayed to the same god as their former colonial masters claimed to worship, the same god who appeared to have sanctioned the 'civilising mission' of the European imperial powers which had resulted in the widespread exploitation of the continent, both of its natural resources and its people. And they seemed eager and determined to show their former teachers and bosses that they had learned their lessons well; that they were not 'primitive' or 'savage' but educated and well-mannered, able to hold their own in 'cultivated' circles and capable of determining their own destinies. My father so revered the high culture of the western world that he had portraits of the great composers on the wall: Beethoven, Mozart, Chopin and Liszt. There didn't appear to be any African composers of note.

My generation grew up questioning those old-school values, and some of us ultimately rejected them. Those values had after all failed to prevent two world wars and the Holocaust; wholesale genocide in South America in the age of the Conquistadors; the Trans-Atlantic slave trade in Africa; the outrage of Apartheid; the savage brutality of the Vietnam War; the continued oppression of African Americans in the United States; and the continuing exploitation of Africa long after the continent's nation states had attained independence. It was impossible to read a history of the colonial experience in Africa and Asia, or the Civil Rights Movement in the US without becoming angry. And if you didn't develop a hard-nosed, cynical attitude towards those in authority, then you were simply naïve and probably deserved to be ripped off by those smart people in Whitehall, Westminster and the City. We learned to doubt everyone and everything. And that cynicism sometimes corroded personal relationships. Trust was not something to be given lightly.

Now that I am middle-aged and a parent myself, I sometimes wonder whether anything has changed: do I appear as old-fashioned and out of touch to you as my parents did to me? They were Analogue to my Digital. I grew up in the Terrestrial Television Age but you are living in the Satellite Internet Age. And I ask myself if I am trying to pass on tastes and values which have no real bearing on the kind of life you're living today? Instead of the great composers, on my

27

walls you will see portraits of Jimi Hendrix, Louis Armstrong, John Coltrane and Miles Davis. (As well as Martin Luther King, Malcolm X and Nelson Mandela). Ever heard of them? You may not even listen to Radio 4 but if this were Desert Island Discs and I offered you The Bible and The Complete Works of William Shakespeare, would you politely accept them? Or would you say "Listen old man, I have no use for either of those books, one written by a white Englishman over four hundred years ago and the other by a bunch of Jewish scribes in a desert. I doubt they're going to help me come to terms with my social isolation and the loneliness of existence in the twenty-first century. What else have you got?"

I've learned to become wary of anyone who passes himself or herself off as some kind of 'guru', dispensing advice on how to live right and achieve success, wealth, serenity or sex appeal. So I'm not about to give you any. It is your task in life to find your own balance between what you think you are as an individual and what you think you ought to be as a member of society. Let me tell you this: I met a guy some years ago who seemed funny, experienced and wise; he was good-natured and easy company. He looked as if he'd had a few ups and downs in life and had learned to look back at it all with wry humour. He wasn't that much older than I was but I wondered what lessons life had taught him. He thought about it for a moment and said 'milk is a meal in itself'. Not the most profound life lesson, I thought but I took him to be echoing that line in the Bob Dylan song: 'Don't follow leaders and watch the parking meters'. In other words, when it comes to the big things in life, be careful whose advice you follow. Either that, or he was working for the Milk Marketing Board.

But if you can't depend on your parents and their generation, or on 'community leaders' or on lifestyle gurus, what's a poor boy supposed to do? Discard all the old maps and blaze his own trail? But if you don't think that there's anything you can usefully learn from older generations, you're likely to end up re-inventing the wheel and making the same mistakes they did. There is a saying that the artist who is self-taught has a very bad teacher. And, face it, you're not likely to get very far up Mount Everest without a good Sherpa. The key question is: how do you spot a good teacher or guide? For blessed indeed is the child who has a good teacher. You know that I'm not just talking about classroom lessons, dress sense or social etiquette. A good teacher can make all the difference between fulfillment and failure: Andy Murray learns from Ivan Lendl and wins Wimbledon. Maria Sharapova appoints Jimmy Connors as her coach and loses. But you may not know if you've been badly taught until years later, by which time it may be too late to win Wimbledon.

I hope that when I die, my kids will be able to inscribe my headstone with 'He Eventually Saw The Wood For The Trees'. I'm not sure that I'm there yet but this much I know: if you are open to guidance and instruction, a good teacher will help you learn how to think, not what to think; a good teacher will admit the limits of their knowledge and seek constantly to learn, even from the young; a good teacher will leave you feeling less cynical about the world without making you feel naive. A good teacher will make you feel more hopeful about the world and your place in it.

And that brings me back to my parents, to all parents who give without taking, who struggle to pass on the right values to children. And the right values are the enduring ones, not just the current ones which match the mood of the times. I believe now that my parents did have a clue about what was going on. The lessons I drew from their lives are the ones I hope to pass on to my own children: a respect for knowledge, reason and discussion, for truth, for learning from experience; a preparedness for taking responsibility for the consequences of my actions; and respect and tolerance for my fellow man and woman. Our sense of right and wrong follows from all that; all that and a good sense of humour. The fact that many fall short of those values doesn't make them any less valid. The attempt to attain them makes us better human beings, capable of living together in some kind of harmony. Love and respect to them, and to you.

Hugh Quarshie

TONY
JARRETT

TO THE FUTURE YOUNG,

I am writing to you as someone society would have considered a child with no future prospects because I was brought up in Tottenham, North London by a single parent. My parents divorce did affect me emotionally when I was at school and I underperformed academically.

But I was not a bad kid at school, because my mum wore the trousers as well as the skirt when it came down to discipline.

But I am here to let you know that there is hope and a future, because we are all born with a talent. You just have to find out what yours is and pursue it with all your heart. There are some things that you will have to put in place so that you can reveal your God-given talent. You have to set the goals that you want to achieve. You may have to make sacrifices, like friendships and socializing, but most of all you will have to work hard and be hungry to reach your goals.

Let me give you an insight into my life as an international athlete. The gift and talent that a man saw in me at a school sports day enabled me to fulfil my dreams and compete at four Olympic Games and win many medals at world championship level.

Life consists of many daily tests. Sometimes you pass them, sometimes you don't.

As an athlete, I lived these tests with particular intensity, as they were my job. A harbinger of my potential and ability; of how my performance would be when it counted the most. I lived very dark moments where I questioned myself and my commitment. Where I over estimated my competitors and allowed myself to be scared by their image.

At the same time there were days when I would beat my own inner, over-optimistic expectations. Days where everyone around would start believing in me, even the most skeptical ones. And I will tell you, there is no greater joy than proving the skeptics wrong; those who put you in a box, set a limit to your potential and scoff at your attempts to make your dream happen. Yes back then my life consisted of an alternation of bad and good moments.

The key to success is to know that whatever you want to become: Olympic athlete, hedge fund manager, doctor, singer or dancer; first, you have to become so inside yourself. Because had I not believed that I was capable of becoming a great athlete, I would have quit either at my first success, out of arrogance, over-optimism (which I have seen happen to many athletes) or at my first failure because of fear (lots of athletes quit out of fear). Instead, I learned that even the most exceptional among us, even the greatest champions have to deal with daily defeats and win. To be a champion means to be so every single day of your life.

We fall many times in our lives. Do you want to know who are the ones who make it? The ones who don't allow success to inebriate them and, (I am saying and), who can spring right back on their feet when defeated, shake hands with their opponents and be ready to challenge them again the next time you meet.

I would leave you with this saying that I tell all the young men I mentor: You are the author of your own life story no matter what background you come from. You are the writer the producer and the director. Make your life story a great piece.

BE THE BEST THAT YOU CAN BE.

Tony Jarrett

SHELDON
THOMAS

DEAR SON

You're right, I have not been around for you, trust me when I tell you it was the streets that turned me into an angry, selfish man and cost me the respect of my son. I hear you ask, like a lone voice crying in the wilderness where is my identity, who will protect me, motivate and inspire me? Where is my father to teach, guide, provide and protect me? I cannot express how much regret I have; I was lost son, lost to the dark demon of these tragic streets, on estates with no way out and no hope.

This is not an excuse, but the truth is your granddad was not there for me either. Don't get me wrong, he did not walk out on me, like I did to you, he was a stubborn man grounded in West Indian tradition, of get an education, become a doctor or a lawyer and life will be great. There was no grey area. He fed and clothed me and he felt that was all he needed to do. On reflection, I understand now that this was as much love as he could give.

I remember being 13 years old when I really needed him to explain to me why young white British men wanted to physically hurt us and hated us being in their country and why he and the Police could not protect us. My dad had no idea what I was going through and was only concerned with keeping a roof over my head, so I looked for someone, anyone, that would listen. Son that was my mistake; I thought the streets was it, but instead I found other lost boys my age, angry, rejected and hurting young men. Just like you, they were looking for answers and guess what, I became their answer. I was a natural leader and even though I was angry, I did not really understand my anger and before I could do anything about it, my anger turned to hatred and this hatred was aimed at white people especially the police. They mentally degraded us by calling us offensive names. Physical beatings by racist officers and the National Front (now known as the BNP), became an everyday experience for most young black boys.

I formed what your generation now calls gangs and this became my mission in life, to take retribution on every racist police officer, and son it did not stop there. When we realised we were just getting locked up, most of us used this as an opportunity to get paid from criminal activity and since the system was not giving us jobs and they disliked us for the colour of our skin, we felt like you, completely justified.

Things changed when I met an MP named Bernie Grant. He was one of four black MPs in the country. He spent three years mentoring me and taught me about black history, racism and how to channel my anger into positive things such as helping the community, producing music and organising business events. He also taught me not to allow my environment and my circumstances to determine what I became. He then took me to the USA to meet the civil rights leader Jesse Jackson who asked me to watch a TV clip of a march he led with Martin Luther King. He asked me what I saw in the TV clip and what I thought the march was about. I told him it was about black people's rights. He explained that it was a message of hope; hope of a better future for all who would believe in change and do their part despite their past. I realised for the first time that just because I was angry, or I felt people hated me, or I felt rejected it was not a reason to become a criminal.

Son, the streets will not help you and even though I know you're hurting right now and feeling angry and rejected, use this opportunity to learn from my mistakes. There is so much more you can do with your life, do not let the roads take control of you. Trust me, anger is one step away from danger, it will either hold you back or kill you. Are you going to allow your anger to determine your outcome?

The streets are a LIE; a concrete jungle where death knocks everyday at the door of another 13 year old black boy, in a parallel world perpetrated by angry young men who use every excuse they can to justify not wanting to be a part of society. All the streets have to offer is greed; lost young men sexually exploiting girls, robbery, fraud, selling and smoking drugs and anything that goes against society. But what you don't realise, is that the root causes of that lifestyle is anger, rejection, absent fathers, struggling mothers, poor education and low self-esteem. Trust me when I tell you, the streets destroy families and once you taste the streets it's very hard to come off them and like some of the people I used to associate with, you become trapped. The streets take you away from your purpose, your destiny; that's why so many black boys never reach their full potential. That does not need to be you. You have so much more to give, you were born to be a success.

If you look down any high street, how many black businesses do you see? How many black headmasters of secondary schools do you hear about? My generation did not set any foundations because a lot of us became trapped on the streets. But you have the chance to change all that. You have the chance to break the cycle that has plagued black men for years. I don't want you to be another statistic; another black boy who does not reach his full potential.

I cannot stress how important it is for you to get your

education. Without it life will be very difficult; it will be the difference between you setting the foundation for reaching your full potential or living a life of subsistence and struggling in a very low paid job.

Right now you are at a crossroads in your life and if you make the right decision now and that includes changing some of your friends, your focus will begin to change. The worst thing in life is living in regret, never reaching your goals, seeing your aspirations never materialise. You only have one life don't make the mistakes so many of your generation have made.

FROM YOUR LOVING FATHER

Sheldon Thomas

EMILE
VIDAL CARR

DEAR YOUNG MAN

Growing up in a West African house with the strictest father in the world was a battle that would definitely shape the man I grew up to be. I was never the most academic of students but one thing that was evident from a young age was that I was highly creative and inquisitive. Naturally I went on to ace my Graphics and Art A-Levels but like most West African fathers, my Dad wanted me to become a lawyer, doctor or both. I moved out of my parents' home two weeks after I finished my last A-Level exam. I only had £30 in my account, but I was so eager to be independent that I wasn't bothered about my lack of finances.

When my Dad found out that I wanted to study fashion I could sense his disappointment. To be honest it also came as a surprise to me, that now at the age of 18 I wanted to study a subject that I used to mock and ridicule when any boy at school took textiles. The first time I got on a sewing machine, working on it felt very natural. I stayed up for two days making a denim suit and the pride I felt overshadowed any hint of tiredness that I was suppressing. I'd found my passion and I was adamant to pursue it.

The earlier in life that you set your ambitions, the more time you will give yourself to master it. Society embraces young people who are gifted and hardworking. Setting an ambition can be quite a difficult thing as you will need to assess your own skills and also what you do and don't like. There are further obstacles once you start the path to your career by form of distractions. Hard working men generally have a modest flock of admiring females that will all be vying for your attention. As a young man you are likely to want to encourage as many of these women as possible but what will happen is that you will slowly become less committed to your work. The best thing to do is put your antennas up and look out for the woman who has similar discipline and ambition to you so that you can both bounce ideas off of each other. Women are very powerful and the right one definitely helps a man to grow, so make her a friend in the beginning and see where things go.

By the age of 24 I was running my own business and my talent enabled me to design clothes that sold in Topshop & ASOS but greed paid for a Chelsea office and a business trip to New York which included staff costs and stays in the Hotel Pennsylvania (Madison Square Garden). This life caught up with me when I got remanded in prison for 4 months because of certain associates I had around me. There I was, another black boy in the dock. My solid upbringing and university degree meant nothing at this point; the CPS tried everything in their power to convict me of a crime that was actually not of my doing. I was released with no charge.

Building standards and earning respect are two things

that take time. Having your own set of standards will help you differentiate yourself from your peers, it helps to mould your decision making. It will aid what kind of people are attracted to your character and values. Respect is an over-used word and many of the younger generation don't truly understand what it means despite wanting it so badly. I have noticed that individuals that I have respect for I have never had to tell them so. Some people respect those that have clean records and as admirable as this may be I also give respect to those who have come back from failure. I revel in the challenge of coming back from moments of personal failure as it not only means you are the underdog but also it gives you an opportunity to come back stronger and it is great to have an opportunity where you can learn from your mistakes.

Even though I grew up in a Christian household it was through this situation that I developed my own relationship with God. My only wish was that it wasn't during the cliché scenario of getting into trouble. I encourage you to discover who Christ is for yourself. He's not just a problem-solver in bad situations; He is life and has given you a purpose.

If I could give you any advice, it would be the following:

Find your passion: Many times I have been up for two, sometimes three days working so that I can meet deadlines, however if I didn't have passion for what I was doing then this would've been more difficult to do. Your passion will be your driving force to succeed when things get tough.

Work hard and work smart: Nothing in this world is worth having if you haven't worked hard for it. By working hard, you will progress and reap honest rewards.

Trust your instincts: Learn to listen to the inner voice about certain situations or individuals. Trust the first decision that you make, as in my experience it has in most cases been the right situation for me.

Be a man of Integrity: In all that you do, do it with honesty, your character will be remembered.

Mentors and Friends: Be careful who you surround yourself with. Move with like minded people who will support, enable and encourage you in your pursuits.

One of the many things that I learnt, is that your character is built up after periods of perceived failure and challenges so don't be afraid to approach them head on. These will be your testimony to encourage others in the same way mine would've hopefully inspired you. My doors are always open to young aspiring individuals, so who knows, we might meet in the near future. For now I wish you many blessings in your endeavours.

YOURS SINCERELY,

Emile Vidal Carr

DAVID
LAMMY

DEAR YOUNG MAN

I have represented Tottenham in Parliament every day for over a decade. It's a job that I am enormously proud to do - representing the place where I grew up, helping it through the good times and the bad. I sometimes have to pinch myself that I have been given this privilege because, growing up, I could not have felt further from the grand hallways and eloquent speeches I often see in the House of Commons.

48

I grew up in the shadow of Broadwater Farm Estate in Tottenham, one of five children in my family. My parents came to London from Guyana, an Afro-Caribbean country in South America. Like most immigrants, they thought that Britain promised a better life for themselves and their family. But when I was just 12 years old, my father left for the USA - and I never saw him again.

Like so many deserted mothers, mine heroically ploughed on, working non-stop to support me and my four siblings. At that time, many of these mothers faced a barrage of insults for apparently failing in their parental duties. Only a few of us truly saw how brave these women were and how well they were doing under the circumstances. Nevertheless, to be fatherless, does leave one with lasting sense of doubt, imperfection and incompleteness. Why did I have one parent, not two, sitting next to me at my school's parents' evening? Why had he decided to abandon us? Had I done something wrong?

Although I made friends and found kind and generous teachers, there were many moments when I struggled to cope with what felt like betrayal by my father. My initial anxieties were predictable: when the first hint of stubble appeared on my face, who would teach me to shave? More problematic were the frustrations that came with living in urban Britain at that time and the mistakes that everyone makes when they are growing up. When I fell, I could not rely on my dad to help pick me up and get me back on my feet.

Many of you will be worrying about the same things, struggling with the same issues that I wrestled with when I was growing up. Keep persevering! Things will get better - I got through those years, and so can you. Even without a father, I still had people who believed in me - my mum, my brother and fantastic teachers. You will have people who believe in you, even if it is sometimes difficult to believe that yourself.

I do, though, worry that things may be even harder for you than they were for me. Today, one in four children is brought up by a lone parent, compared with one in 14 in 1972, the year I was born. Lone parents are some of the unsung heroes of this country - I know that my mum was. But nobody can say that life is easy for them or for the children that they struggle so hard to bring up well.

I have two sons just a few years younger than you. I love my sons more than anything else in this world and I am constantly trying to be the best father I can be for them. My sons are probably a lot like you. They are bright, inquisitive and caring. I only wish the rest of the world saw my boys in the same way. Sadly, when many people look at my sons, they do not see the wonderful traits that they will use to someday contribute to Britain and the world. Instead, they simply see their physical appearances.

I wish I could tell my sons - and you - that all you need to succeed in this world is to try your best. Unfortunately, at this moment in our history, young black boys cannot rely on just trying their best. You cannot merely be as good as your peers. You must be better. You must try harder than you imagine possible, and you must rely on the help and guidance of people who want the best for you. You must not blame others when you don't succeed - learn from your challenges, your mistakes and your failures and come back better next time.

I had to learn this myself when I was your age.

When I won a choral scholarship to The King's School in Peterborough, I was suddenly removed from the familiarity of Tottenham and rocketed into an environment where I was the only black student.

Many believed my future would be determined by where I came from. They believed if your appearance fits a certain stereotype or if you live in a certain postcode you will not succeed. People expected me to fail. My only response to this was to work. And unfortunately, to work as hard as my peers would not be enough to shake off the label many people had placed on me. I would need to prove that I could do more than just take part; I needed to prove that I could excel.

It was thanks to the help of my mother, and my larger community that I was able to succeed. This love and support aided me as I went from boarding school to study law in London, and eventually to earn a Masters in Law at Harvard Law School in America.

Thankfully, growing up without a father didn't mean I had to lower my sights. I had an older brother who looked after me. Teachers, priests and youth workers all stepped in to fill the great father-shaped hole in my life. I never forgot the hole that he left, but as the months and years went by, I stopped it holding me back and used it to spur me on. If you are facing the same hole in your life, you can do the same. It won't be easy, but if I can do it, then so can you.

Whether you grew up with two loving parents, or, like me, with just one hard-working parent, it is vitally important that you seek out mentors and role models. No matter what you want to do when you grow up, there are adults that have valuable experiences from which you can learn. Ask questions - and be sure to listen to the answers. If you are willing to learn, I can promise you that there are many people willing to teach you.

You must find your own mentors and father figures. Even if you do have a supportive mum and dad, every additional role model you find will contribute another valuable lesson to your upbringing. After all, it takes a village to raise a child. Some children are born lucky enough to have this village already available to them at birth. Some must work hard for it. Still others are born into really awful, difficult circumstances. In Tottenham, many children grow up without the basic things so many people take for granted - enough to eat, a safe home in which to sleep, or even a loving mum and dad.

These situations are incredibly sad and terribly unfair. But children in these situations cannot simply give up. I did not have an easy childhood, and what I learned from it is that overcoming hard situations is a choice. Removing yourself from these tough situations takes both a willingness to seek out mentors and a lot of personal resilience. Developing this resilience early in life will only make you a stronger, more successful adult.

I hope that life treats you as well as it can. Take whatever luck you can find, but don't rely on it - make your own luck. Take whatever advice and help people can offer, but don't rely on them - make your own way in life.

I can't promise that it will be easy - it almost certainly won't be. But it can be fun and you can go through life without regrets if you stay true to yourself and live up to your own expectations. You will sometimes fall; I certainly did. But if you can pick yourself up and dust yourself off,

54

I promise you will be proud of what you have achieved. I wish you all the very best of luck as you start your way in life.

David Lammy
MEMBER OF PARLIAMENT FOR TOTTENHAM

CLINTON JORDAN

DEAR FRIEND,

I know growing up in the type of world we live in is not easy.

I remember a few years ago sitting with my friends - predominantly black males - and reflecting on how difficult it had been growing up. But listening to these guys talk about how hard it was to be 'black', how hard it was to be a pure ethnic race, typically African or West Indian, I realised that I didn't actually fit into either of those categories. I realised that it was one thing growing up as a young 'black boy', but what about growing up as a mixed race child? After trying so many different ways of living up to the expectations of those from my race, or other people's opinions of my race I decided one thing: 'Clinton, just be you.'

You know, one of the hardest things to be is the one standing in front of the mirror. You.

I don't know if you're like me when I was young, but do you spend quite a lot of your time trying to be like someone else? A celebrity sports star or hero maybe? In fact, I know this might sound funny, but do you spend a lot of your time being like your race? If that's you I would like to ask you one thing. What is 'being a black man' supposed to be like? I mean there's no set of instructions or manual that come with our skin colour. In fact who gave you the name Black? I think names are very important; names give life. So before we accept the name, you need to ask yourself what is its purpose? Do you match that name?

There is a person inside of you that is itching to get out, but the only person that is in the way of you, is that someone else that you are trying to be. Have you ever liked your best friend's jacket, trainers or cap, asked to try on, and then looked in the mirror and didn't like what you saw? That's the way we are in life with people. Sometimes we try on their character, we might try to wear their swagger but it just doesn't seem to fit. My advice to you is to take yourself on a little journey. Take some time out to discover you. You'll be surprised what taking a little time out does for you.

Ain't it funny that the one lesson that they don't have in school, the one course that they don't have at college, the only degree that you can't study at university is 'how to be you'? Yet we are not given much time in our life to study 'me'. This means that there are a high percentage of people out in the world that have not put time aside to find out what 'me' is all about.

Maybe if I studied 'me', I could be free of uncertainty and insecurity, and vulnerability! (LOL!)

Just by putting a little time in to study 'me' could free you from the uncertainty of being accepted in society. Be bold and confident that there is no other you. Hurry! you need to know 'you' before others do!

And just by putting a little timing into studying 'me', could free you from the insecurities that the history of your skin contains. You don't have to worry about being the only black guy in this school, in this job, in this institution, or in this town, say "I AM ME! and you should be glad I AM HERE!"

And just by putting a little time into studying 'me', will free you from being vulnerable in a relationship of any kind, whether it be your best friend, girlfriend, wife, mother, father, boss or foe, or maybe you will be the boss and have the ability to help other vulnerable people too. Say 'It's GREAT to be me'.

Because of my dual heritage I have had very mixed opinions on who I am. I say 'opinions' as I used to rely heavily on what other people thought about me, because I couldn't figure it out myself. So, because of the mixed opinions in my life, I spent most of my youth feeling a bit dizzy. Trying to get a hold of your identity as a young man is very hard. Trying to get a hold of your identity as a young black man is even harder. But trying to get hold of your identity as a young man from mixed ethnic heritage - well, think about how hard that was!

I decided to let go of my skin. One of the turning

points came when I found myself in the Accident &
Emergency department of a local hospital one day. I was
in the queue and behind the screen was an Asian woman
taking the details of all of the soon be patients. She greeted
me and said, 'Name please?'

'Clinton Jordan,' I replied.

'Age?' she asked.

'36,' I said

'Ethnicity?' she went on to question.

'What do you mean?' I chose as a cheeky response.
I really don't like those questions on the forms.

'Where do you come from?' the woman said peering
through the glass barrier.

'England.'

'No, I mean what nationality?' pointing to the table of
nationalities on her form.

I challenged her 'How would you define the nationality
you come from. Your mother or your father?'

'That would be your father,' she said.

So I smiled at her and said 'My nationality is Indian.' She
looked at me very puzzled because all she could see was

'black' skin. It was at that time that I realised that people want skin colour to have something to do with what ever you are going through but the truth is it doesn't have anything to do with anything. Not if you don't want it to.

You are what YOU say you are regardless of colour, shape or ethnicity. What you see is what you will be.

Try this today my young friend. Stand in front of the mirror and ask yourself 'will I spend a lifetime fighting for the existence of my skin, or will I spend a lifetime fighting for the existence of my unique purpose that will stand in the hallway of eternity for all to see?'

Wait for your answer. Wait for it . . .

A Friend

Clinton Jordan

CLEON
WILSON

DEAR YOUNG MAN,

Thursday 15 2013 August aka A-Level Results Day!

I write to you as a big brother, wanting only the very best for you.

I find it interesting that I have started to put this letter together on a day that separates the 'men from the boys!' I really see today as a day of reckoning for some young men who may or may not have put a lot of hard work into their A-Level studies. How did you or your people do? Was today a proud moment or a moment of cold, harsh 'oh boy, I got what I worked for' reality?

I remember being 'you' when I was younger, it wasn't long ago - I'm only 34!

I was raised well and into a big extended family in Hackney. Trust me, Hackney was laid back, relaxed and drama free during the late 1980s and I liked where I lived. I also enjoyed my primary and secondary school days - secondary school a bit too much!! :(

If I learnt nothing else during my time at secondary school, it was to work real hard (do you really want to be an average man?) and play real hard too! That lesson was like a humongous happy slap in the face when I got my GSCE results!! You see before that fateful date in August 1996, I was oblivious to the reality that was fast approaching my front door. How could I have ever thought that I would pass all my GCSEs when I spent most of my time chilling (until I almost froze), laughing, joking and not studying very hard at all.

Let me break it down for you. I was raised by a single mother who worked a regular job as a secretary and struggled to raise me on her own. I was blessed with an amazing opportunity to study at a phenomenal secondary boarding school in West Sussex. Some kids from the boarding school knew the Headmaster at my primary school in Hackney so they came down one day and told all the year 6 kids about the school. That was a once in a lifetime moment for me, so I made it my business to get into the school no matter what the cost; and boy it did cost my mum in terms of money, time, effort and everything else. But, it cost me too. I had to get some private tuition to prepare me for the entrance exam which I flopped on the first attempt. Thank God I got in second time round and then I arrived in a place I had never, ever seen before in my life. Acres of green grass, fresh country air and the opportunity to be something big!

But the SAD PART is that I didn't really appreciate that at the time! So instead I messed around in class, I put in very little effort with my schoolwork and I had way too much fun and jokes! I had no mentor, TA, Head of Year or anyone else to say to me: "Cleon fix up!" My God, I wish I did have someone who could have just said that to me - I believe I would have come back to my senses and had a change of mind.

The question is will you man up? You may or may not think that right now you're already fixed. 'Well, I don't get in any trouble with the police.' I didn't either. 'I don't get many/ any detentions.' Well done. Neither did I.

But, I still say that you need to 'man up.' You need to study more, work more, think more, plan more, dream more, know more, laugh more, play more, take more and give more! I encourage you to man up to all the responsibilities in your young life because no one can live your life for you but you and you do it best!

So please, please, please withdraw your membership from the school of losers and jokers and stay in the school for hard workers, risk takers and winners.

So come on, the first step is always the scariest but it's not the hardest one to take. When you break it down, it's really only about forming new habits and staying on track; have a goal or vision in mind and pursue it with all your heart, with all your soul and with all your strength.

I just read an article from The Voice Newspaper talking about a young black boy who was a Mathematics genius at the age of 12. He WORKED hard for an A* grade and

65

after stating that he had a natural aptitude for Maths, his comment was: 'still had to do a bit of work!' Did you get that? He still had to do a bit of work! May I encourage you to have the same attitude, to never be settled for second best or a substitute position. Good old-fashioned hard work will NEVER, EVER go out of fashion - trust me. Don't learn it the hard way like I did!

The final thought that I want to leave with you is this:

Anyone can be a nobody, a bum, a wasteman, a gangster etc. but if you want to be the best you can be and do it better than your dad, older brother, granddad or uncle ever did, then it WILL TAKE hard work, determination and a mindset that will not take no for the final answer and will only be content with 1st place!

So forget the saying: 'it's not the winning but the taking part that counts,' because believe me you have to win in this game to be successful.

So young man, remember that I've written to you as a big brother wanting only the very best for you.

Cleon Wilson

TONY
HARRISON

DEAR FRIEND

My name is Tony, and for the last 20 years I have been creating and delivering bespoke training programmes and seminars focused on human development. What that means is that I have helped and supported 1000's of people to find a way to live the best life they can and get the most out of the opportunities and challenges that life has to offer them.

There's something really special about seeing people change based on the development and the strengthening of their minds. Just like when you're pumping iron at the gym; you feel that burn on your muscles and it hurts like hell, but then a few weeks later you feel the hardening of that muscle and people start to say how good you look. It's the same with your thoughts; when you start to become observant, listening and learning from the mistakes and successes of other people rather than blindly repeating their experiences, you start to find that you become more confident and capable in the things you attempt and believe it or not you also become more successful!

I wish you were here right now, in front of me. Why? Because it's always easier to understand what someone means when you can see their eyes and right now I want you to see my eyes because I want to share some thoughts with you. They are not thoughts telling you what to do. No, that decision is up to you. The choices we make in life will determine the way we are treated, seen and understood by other people. That's just a fact, so my first suggestion to you is that in all things choose wisely.

So where do I start. I guess a good place is to explain why I am writing to you.

The world is changing; I've seen it happen in front of my eyes. It's weird because even though the changes occur it can almost feel that nothing is really happening and then before you know it you have fallen behind in the game of life. The greatest advancement in the world over the last, say 20 years, is the global communication and information sharing system, commonly known as the Internet. It is the technology that has turned average people into billionaires, many of them before they reach the age of 30 (think Facebook and Twitter). It is also the tool that has given ordinary people the ability to research and acquire information that has changed their lives forever. That said there are also many people that have access to this phenomenal tool and fail to use it in a way that benefits their growth and development. These same people then complain that they didn't get a chance in life or that they haven't achieved what they wanted to in life because no one gave them that chance. Know this, achievers don't wait to be given anything, they go and seek their success and fortune in whatever form or shape it may come in. So don't wait to be given an opportunity, be entrepreneurial and make things happen.

Knowledge is a powerful tool, but knowledge without wisdom can turn a man into a fool and you are nobody's fool, remember that! The fact that you know this is not enough unfortunately. In life you must always aim to create the outcome that you want, you should be in control, even of the things that ultimately have other people making the final decision. Don't feel powerless or that someone else is controlling you.

Understand that the way you present yourself may heavily influence that final decision. You can't act in a negative way and expect to be treated positively. For example, would you think someone is an eloquent speaker if all they do is cuss when they are talking? Act how you want to be treated and the funny thing is that the more you do that is the less you realise your doing it. It will become your positive habit.

So, I have a question for you; what would you do if I gave you some advice?

Would you follow it? Would you ignore it? Hopefully neither.

I hope that initially you would test it, prove it to be true, prove it to be right for you. I don't want you to be a follower that does something just because they've been told to. I am not a pied piper with a band of merry creatures following me to wherever I am going. Yes I am wise, experienced and to some degree knowledgeable, but all these attributes relate to the life I live and the world I live in, which may not resemble or look like yours. This is why I need you not to just accept what you're told in life (initially) but to first ask yourself questions;

- Do I trust the source of this advice?
- Do I understand what this person is telling me?
- Have I explained myself clearly to the person advising me, do they get me and what I'm trying to do here?

Does this make sense?

I'm almost sure that at this stage of your life people are always giving you advice of some type and maybe you listen; maybe you don't.

I'm going to share a very true story with you. Some time ago I was mentoring a young man; he had come to the UK from another country at a very young age. His opportunities in the UK were limited because he was brought here under a false identity (I don't judge his parents for this, they were trying to give their son a chance in life that they never had for themselves.) The one message the parents continually shared with him was 'stay away from trouble', you never know when it may come back to bite your backside! He didn't listen and unfortunately started rolling with the wrong crowd, getting involved in silly little things that could have been avoided. But because they seemed fun at the time he just went ahead with whatever his friends were doing. This got him a petty criminal record, which almost led to him being deported from the UK. As with most people as he grew older he began to see the error of his ways and started to clean up his act, knuckling down in college and creating positive opportunities for himself. He found a girl-friend and had a child, life looked good and people started to praise him about the way he had made this change and encouraged him to just keep doing the right thing; the good news is that's exactly what he did. He worked harder and then he worked harder still to make up for the lost time and opportunities. This individual was also creatively a very talented musician and during this period had begun to attract the attention of various record labels both in the UK and abroad. One particular very well known recording company decided they wanted to sign him and give him something that rarely happens now and that was a multiple album deal. Put simply this opportunity was about to take him from claiming tax credit to survive, to living a millionaire lifestyle. All he had to do was fly to USA to sign the contract THAT'S ALL!

What happened next is ridiculous. Because he did not have a British passport he had to get a full visa from the American Embassy, but before he could get that he had to declare any criminal activity. Once he told them that he had been arrested in the past for some silly mistakes when he was younger, they did a full check on his past. They found out that one of the silly things he had done was handle a stolen credit card. He didn't even steal it; someone else did. But what he did do was handle the card, therefore he became party to the theft and under joint enterprise, he was as guilty as the person who actually stole the card.

The only reason they both got caught was because they stupidly brought £5 credit top up for their mobile phones. This one thing on his police records led to him not getting the visa issued!!! This then led to the record company rethinking the opportunity they were offering. They began thinking that if he could not travel freely, then how was he going to be able to come to the USA to work with producers, songwriters, or do shows. The bottom line is that they withdrew the offer. He never did get to sign that contract and ultimately he became disillusioned with the entertainment industry and stopped making music.

He now lives in regret and for a while became very bitter and angry, but who could he blame? Only himself. By now you're probably feeling really sorry for this guy, why? Because ultimately he lost his life opportunity for a £5 mobile phone credit! Even though he had turned a corner and was making people proud, his past caught up with him and a great opportunity was snatched from the palm of his hand.

So what's the message I'm leaving with you? It's a very basic one. Avoid the temptation at this stage of your life to do things that have the possibility of coming back to snatch future opportunities out of the palm of your hand. Do not allow yourself to live in regret; I do not want this for you. Learn from other people's mistakes and do not become the lesson that someone else has to learn from.

Remember, always to have a dream that you can turn into a goal, something that you can work towards, something that means so much to you that when you're tempted to not give a damn and do the wrong thing, it's strong enough to make you think twice. So I end this short letter the same way I started it; life is always going to present circumstances and situations to you, both good and bad but ultimately your achievements and successes will be measured by the choices you make. So choose wisely knowing that you can be the master of your destiny.

I really wish you well.

PS: When you make it to the top of your tree and you're living good, look me up, I'd love to hear how you did it.

PEACE.
Tony Harrison

MAC
ATTRAM

DEAR YOUNG MAN

So you want to be a success in business? Great! Don't let anyone talk you out of it.

In order to be a success in anything, you have to have a winning mind-set. There are two little voices that you will battle with in everything that you do in life. There is a voice that says that 'you can't' and a voice that says that 'you can'. The biggest battle you face is telling yourself that you can and shutting out any voice that tells you that you can't.

Still not convinced that you can make it big in business? The following are examples of people like you that did.

GEORGE CRUM (BORN: 1822. DIED: 1914)

Unbeknownst to many, George Crum invented the world's first potato chip; and he was black.

The potato chip industry now generates billions of dollars every year. Mr. Crum was a chef who hailed from Saratoga Springs, New York and invented the potato chip almost by accident in 1853. He had served French fries to a customer who complained that they were too thick, so he made a much thinner version with a little seasoning for the customer and the potato chip was born. The simple potato chip was an instant hit and was distributed on a wider scale in 1920, 6 years after the death of George Crum. The invention of the potato peeler helped to facilitate the mass roll out of the potato chip and George Crum's legacy lives on today.

Why was Mr. Crum so successful? He solved a problem; successful business people and inventors solve problems.

BEN CARSON (BORN: 1951)

Ben Carson is a gifted

neurosurgeon who astounded the world by becoming the first surgeon to successfully separate conjoined twins.

His work has revolutionised the medical field and he has secured his place in history. His single mother raised Mr Carson and he struggled with anger management issues as a child. However, his mother instilled a strict discipline on him, making him read 2 books a week as a teenager. As a result of his determination Mr Carson graduated with flying colours from high school and worked hard to develop a career in neurosurgery. To date, Ben Carson has been awarded 38 honorary doctorate degrees and he has many accolades.

Why did Ben Carson succeed? He had an incredible talent and committed himself to a lifelong programme of learning; successful people are constantly learning and honing their skill.

ALEXANDER AMOSU (BORN: 1974) Alexander Amosu is a British born Nigerian entrepreneur who has excelled in the business world.

Entrepreneurialism runs in Mr. Amosu's blood. At the age

of 16, he was successfully promoting basketball tournaments and club nights in his spare time. Amosu started a home cleaning agency at the age of 19, which quickly accumulated a turnover of £4,000 within a few months of starting. He ran the business whilst completing his studies and discontinued it 3 years later.

Alexander Amosu's significant breakthrough came at the age 25, when he combined his love for technology with business. In 1999, Mr Amosu founded the company RnB Ringtones, which was the first urban ringtone company in Europe. Recognising a gap in the market, Mr Amosu created the company and promoted it on the back of flyers. Word spread very quickly and Alexander Amosu found the orders flooding in. The company did so well that it turned over £1 million within its first year of trading, making Mr. Amosu a millionaire at the age of 25.

He later sold the company for a huge profit and has gone on to make his mark in the luxury goods market. He sells products that include; bespoke suits, mobile phones and champagne. Alexander Amosu recently launched OK! Magazine in Nigeria and his clients include high profile celebrities worldwide.

Why has Alexander Amosu succeeded? He tried several business ventures and he persevered until he discovered what worked for him; successful people keep on going, even when things get difficult.

We can learn so much from the people mentioned above and I have a lot of experience to share from my own business ventures. There are some vital components that I believe are part of the success DNA and I believe that you cannot attain business success without them.

- *Do what you love.* If I were to ask you what your passion is, what would you say? The truth is that successful people focus on what they love doing. Alexander Amosu loved technology and he made over a million pounds from it.

  Personally, I love to train and motivate people. It's my passion and I have created a successful business from it as a result. When you love what you do, work no longer seems boring. Sure, you need to treat it like a business and you need to be business minded to a certain extent, but that can be learned. Passion can't.

When you love what you do, it comes across to your clients. It also motivates you to keep on going through the good and the bad. You are never too young to identify your passions. I have always loved motivating people and it was something that I did even in the school playground. However, because I was unaware that training was my passion, I tried other things before coming back to it.

You are in an ideal position because you can identify what you love right now and you can pursue it relentlessly.

Become a leader. If you are not leading, you are following and it may not be in the direction that you wish. Strong business people are powerful leaders. They don't follow the latest trends or crowds; they create them.

- Arrogance is not the same as leadership. Leadership means having personal goals, a sense of direction and not allowing yourself to be easily influenced by others.

Are you willing to focus on your future whilst your peers may be focusing on leisurely activities? Are you willing to set goals on a regular basis and review them? Are you willing to take responsibility for where you are now and where you want to go? Can you put a plan in motion in order to get there?

If the answer is yes then you are ready to be a leader. It does not have to be hard. In fact, goal setting is fun, particularly when you are doing something that you enjoy.

- *Develop good, wholesome qualities.* In order to succeed in business, there are certain characteristics that must be ingrained within you and you are in an ideal position to foster these characteristics. Successful business people have:

    INTEGRITY
    HONESTY
    RESPECTFULNESS
    PATIENCE

It may go without saying but in business, reputation is everything. Your reputation will take you further than your business card ever will. If you are known as an arrogant person, people will not want to do business with you. If you are dishonest, people definitely will not want to do business with you. You are in an ideal position to consciously develop these characteristics.

Good manners go a long way in life, and the same can be applied in business.

If you want to be successful in business, read books by people who have reached the top of their field; look at their successes, look at their failures and learn from them. If you are not a huge fan of reading or if you are always on the move, use audio books. There is nothing stopping you from becoming great in your field. The main obstacle is what you tell yourself.

Conquer your self-talk and you can conquer anything.

Mac Attram

EJIKE
O WODU

DEAR YOUNG MAN,

Writing a letter with a cause to young men can have one of two effects: Inspiration or rebellion.

People of any age have a way of responding to information depending on the way it is presented. So I present this letter to you without shouting, without preaching and without judgement.

If you read it and it has the slightest positive impact on your life, I would have done something useful for you and for the world as a whole.

We have been afforded the freedom to choose how we live our lives. This includes how we make our money, what we wear and how we eat at a dinner table. Some think they are burdened with restriction. We are not. We have to make the most of our numerous options. This is a freedom some cannot boast.

Restriction comes in many guises but in the UK, restriction exists only in a fraction of our endeavours. Detroit, Michigan, in the USA in 2013 is an example of a society where men and women of all ages are almost totally not free. This is not because they are enslaved, but simply because there is nothing in the city. When I say nothing, I mean nothing. No jobs because there are no shops or industries. No money because there are no banks and no one has a job. No salary equals no spending; no spending means a business has no customers and so on. There are not many houses left and the ones that are left are derelict. Images of Detroit, a once thriving city, are reminiscent of scenes from the movie '*I Am Legend*'. Yes, the place has turned to a forest with trees growing out of houses.

Now is the time of plenty, and there is enough of the

pie for everyone to take a bite. I was born in 1974 which is not that long ago. During my time growing up, there was no way I could cut a record deal and become number one in the charts in the space of a week.

Start-up loans for small business were much harder to come by. The Internet was in its infancy. YouTube was non-existent.

My point is that there is so much opportunity out there, to miss it would be a travesty. And we have access to money. Although I would avoid benefits as much as possible, they are there to keep us from abject poverty. But many countries do not have this cushion.

Knowing this and knowing I have family abroad (roughly my age, some younger) that have nothing, made me really think. No money, no jobs, and no access to these things. Yet they get up every day fighting. Fighting with a plan of how to survive.

One of them managed to get a working visa to the UK and put me to shame. He worked a pretty menial job or three and saved £15,000 in about 18 months. At the time, I was overdrawn by about £2,500. If you asked me how, it was because I took life and access to money for granted. I fooled myself with credit cards. I could have paid them off, but chose to delay and delay until the debts compounded.

I'm in a very good place now, with good money in the bank, but it took me way too long to get here.

I'll summarise things I would love you to take away with you if anything.

- *Volition:* We have freedom of choice. Use it.
- *Luck:* This can be defined as when preparation meets opportunity. Be prepared.
- *Act:* The world is your stage. Perform. Every human that wakes up in the morning puts on a costume and goes out to make people believe they are who they say they are. Lawyers do it and so do I when I'm in the boardroom.
- *Dream:* Nothing in this world was or will be without the dreams and imagination of mankind.
- *Plan:* A French saying goes as follows, 'A man with no plan has the same destination as a dead leaf being blown by the wind.'
- *Handsfree:* A tough one, but if you are

harbouring any issues, try to drop or address them. Example, a person goes into a new relationship with issues from a previous relationship (baggage). How can that person embrace the new person with all that heavy baggage? Drop it.

Having free hands will also allow you to grab the opportunities that are presented to you.

Finally, imagine some bad acquaintances as lead weights and some good ones as free floating spirits. The bad ones will pull you down. The good ones will lift you up. But remember, that the force of gravity is far greater than the force of lift. Choose wisely.

Mr Ejike O Wodu

Biographies

MAC
ATTRAM

Mac had many years of challenges and failures in business before discovering what really works!

His tenacity and over 30 years of Martial Arts practice helped him stay focussed and disciplined; a trait he takes into all areas of his life including business.

Over the last 14 years he has developed and sold

several profitable companies. He is a multi-award winning business coach and author, and has been featured as an 'expert advisor' in TV, newspapers and magazines.

In 2013 he was awarded the 'Executive Coach of the Year' in the UK.

He is the Co-founder of SalesPartners UK, helping business owners increase their sales revenues, implement better processes, and build winning business teams; so that they can have more time off to enjoy their lives.

The principles he learned in business and now teaches to others helped him earn millions for himself and now for his clients.

CONTACT:
Mac@MacAttram.com
www.MacAttram.com

EMILE
VIDAL CARR

Emile Carr is a 28 year old graduate from the prestigious London College of Fashion. At the age of 18 he started to sew and shortly after completing his degree set up a high street brand called Bellanina that went on to sell products to Topshop and ASOS. During this time the company was chosen as one of a handful of British designers to go and represent homegrown talent at New York Fashion Week 2008. After the recession Carr took the uncanny step of setting up a high end brand called 'Emile' whilst at the same time taking on technical roles at Alexander McQueen, Peter Pilotto and Erdem for a couple seasons.

JULIAN
GOLDING

Julian Golding's International career began as a junior in 1993-1994 winning the sprint double for 100m and 200m at the National Junior Championships. He then represented Great Britain at the World Junior Championships finishing 8th in the 100m, and winning Gold in the 4x100m relay.

   Julian made steady progress through the seniors,

but came to prominence by winning the 200m at the European U23's Championships in 1997. He then anchored the British team winning a Bronze medal at the 1997 World Championships, in Athens

Julian has gone on to win medals at numerous International competitions, but his crowning glory came, when in Kuala Lumpur, he floated to a personal best of 20.18sec for the 200m, winning the Gold medal at the Commonwealth Games, and a second Gold in the 4x100m relay.

Julian was part of Team GB's 4 x 100 metre relay team at the 2000 Summer Olympics in Sydney, but the team were disqualified in the first round. He failed to qualify for his preferred event, due to illness at the Olympic Trials.

Julian's last major competition was in 2003, where he represented Great Britain at the Paris World Championships. Three years later, he was forced to retire prematurely, due to persistent injuries.

On 18 July 2012, Julian graduated from Middlesex University with First Class Honours for Sports and Exercise Science with Teaching & Coaching. He now a teacher of Physical Education.

TONY HARRISON

Tony Harrison was born and raised in south London a child to Jamaican parents who worked hard under difficult circumstances to keep the family together. Losing his mother while still a teenager Tony lost his most important role model before he was ready to take on independence. This caused him to struggle in becoming the man he is today, and that struggle defines the man he has become. Tony is now a social entrepreneur. For the last 15 years he has specialised in human development through the creation and facilitation of bespoke training programmes and products. He has delivered and trained many organisations and individuals quite simply in how to get the best and most out of life.

A founding member of the 100 Black Men of London, Co Founder of Black Men in the Community, Director of Youth in Excellence and Black Youth Achievements, it is clear that Tony has a passion for what happens within the Black community but for him he also believes that excellence amongst the community should not be the best kept secret! He can often be found advocating on behalf of young people, families and communities within the political and commercial corridors of power, opening channels of opportunity that may otherwise be missed.

Tony has spent time working as a behavioural consultant and mediator within the education system and challenges the excessive illegal use of exclusions within our changing academic teaching system.

Known for his direct but nurturing approach Tony smiles

as he says 'there is no greater feeling than being stopped by someone who you do not recognise who reminds you that you used to mentor or coach them and it was those words that you shared with them that has allowed them to become the person they are today.'

CONTACT:

www.youthinexcellence.com

www.blackyouthachievements.com

www.gkconsultancy.com

REVEREND
LES ISAAC

Born in Antigua, Les moved to the UK as a young child in 1965, growing up in north London with his parents. He experienced gangs and street violence in his teens, becoming a Rastafarian in his search for hope. Then in his late teens Les became a Christian. This radical life changing experience inspired him to always seek ways to engage with the same hard-to-reach communities that he came from. Committed to sharing not only the spiritual relevance of the gospel message, but also the very practical message of the gospel of Jesus Christ.

Les is married to Louise and they have two grown children. He has been a minister for over 30 years and is currently an associate minister of the Christian Life Fellowship in Greenwich London. He is Chief Executive Officer of Ascension Trust which he founded 20 years ago 'out of his concern to see churches involved in mission relevant to their own context and locality'. He was awarded an OBE in the Queen's birthday honours list in 2012 for his work as Head of Ascension Trust. Les founded the Street Pastors Initiative 10 years ago in response to the growing concern for the problems of gun and knife crime, binge drinking, gang culture, loneliness, violence and fear within our communities.

Les is the author of three books, *Dreadlocks*, *Relevant Church* and *Street Pastors*.

TONY
JARRETT

Anthony Alexander Jarrett is a former sprint and hurdling athlete. Jarrett's personal best time for the 110m hurdles is 13.00 seconds, set when he finished as runner-up to Colin Jackson at the 1993 World Championships. Between 1988 and 2003 Tony was an international 110m hurdler representing GB and competed in four Olympic Games.

Jarrett came 4th in the 110m hurdles at the 1992 Summer Olympics in Barcelona, missing a bronze medal by 1000th of a second to Jack Pierce of the USA. He has amassed a plethora of medals over ten years, making him one of Team GB's most successful athletes.

Even though an Olympic medal eluded him, his medals come from highly competitive events such as IAAF World Indoor Championships, World Championships, and European Games amongst others.

Since 2006, Jarrett has been a scout finding potential athletes, whilst mentoring and giving advice to young aspiring athletes. Within education in east London, Jarrett has successfully worked on one-to-one sessions with students motivating them to reach their full potential.

Tony Jarrett is now in demand in the media for his opinion, achievements and expertise. In 2013 he appeared on the BBC Breakfast programme where he shared his experiences with viewers on Usain Bolt's disqualification at the 100m final at the World IAAF Championship in South Korea. Jarrett was also featured as a coach to rising stars on BBC's promotional video for London Olympics 2012. He

102

is also a regular feature on Channel 4's Para-Olympic Show.

Tony Jarrett continues to motivate sports and non-sports people around the UK. This former champion is not resting on his laurels. Whatever young people want to be, Jarrett never fails to inspire, motivate and create future champions and leaders - he coins his well known phrase 'BELIEVE IN YOUR TALENT!'

CLINTON JORDAN

Clinton Jordan is the Director of 'Jordan Music Workshops' (JMW), a family company whose mission is to raise standards through music workshops using the tools of vocal ensemble workshops and instrumental tuition.

JMW's focus is to help People's music awareness.

Clinton is a Jack Petchey Award Winner for 'Outstanding

Leader' for his musical influence and mentoring of young people.

Clinton is the eldest of 8 children all of whom are musical and who, alongside their parents, form 'The Jordan Family,' renowned for their inspirational contribution to the gospel industry. Clinton also runs 'J/FLY', an independent family run record label, 'St Annes' recording studio and leads the evangelism department at Bethesda Ministries, UK. He has been married to Jeannette for 15 years and they have 3 children.

Clinton spent his early years touring the world with the London Community Gospel Choir (LCGC) when he learnt to hone his skills on harmonic awareness, and has sung with artists such as Mariah Carey, Celine Dion and Tina Turner, but to name a few. Clinton later on went into teaching, in his early twenties, and was mentored under the tutelage of Music Ethnomusicologist Dr Krzysztof Ćwiżewicz.

DAVID
LAMMY

David Lammy is the Labour MP for Tottenham, the place where he grew up and where much of his family still lives. When he first won his seat, he was 27 and was the youngest MP in the House of Commons. He was a Government Minister for nine years, including Minister for Higher Education from 2008 until 2010. Before entering politics, he worked as a lawyer in London and practised for a year in Los Angeles, after studying at Harvard Law School. He is the author of 'Out Of The Ashes: Britain After The Riots.'

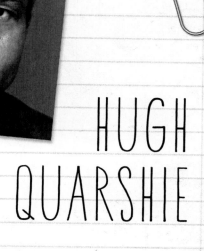

HUGH
QUARSHIE

Hugh Quarshie has become known for his many appearances in the long-running BBC medical drama, Holby City. Many years ago, he once played a leading role in a Star Wars movie; and many more years ago, he was a leading member of the Royal Shakespeare Company. He is waiting for a knighthood to revive his movie career. Born in Ghana, educated in London, Cheltenham and Oxford, he won Celebrity Mastermind in 2004.

SHELDON THOMAS

Sheldon Thomas is the Founder and CEO of Gangsline. An inspirational and pioneering individual, Sheldon has an unprecedented insight into gangs through his own experience as a leading gang member in the 1970s. He now dedicates his life to engaging directly with gang leaders and members, using a 'no holds barred', yet spiritual, approach to changing gang members' lives.

His journey began in 1988 when he met the late Bernie Grant, former Labour MP for Tottenham. Bernie saw great potential in Sheldon and offered to mentor him. In the subsequent years Sheldon used his new found focus as he travelled to areas of the United States and Jamaica where he met civil rights activists Jesse Jackson, and to learn all he could about gang and drug related violence and how they tackle it.

Sheldon is a motivational speaker and visionary and is contacted weekly across the globe by individuals, businesses and government representatives who seek expert advice on gang culture which is blighting communities and is failing to be successfully addressed by politicians and criminologists alike. Sheldon has been married for fourteen years and has four children. Sheldon has a BA degree in marketing and combined studies and certificate and diploma in management.

CONTACT DETAILS AND SOCIAL SITES

GANGSLINE, Fortis House, Suite 302 - 303, 160 London Road, Barking, IG11 8BB

TEL: 0208 2141100

EMAIL ADDRESS: enquiries@gangsline.com

WEBSITE: www.gangsline.com

FACEBOOK:

https://www.facebook.com/sheldon.thomas3?ref=tn_tnmn

http://www.facebook.com/pages/

Gangsline/155239217850509

http://www.linkedin.com/pub/sheldon-thomas/16/321/985

http://www.youtube.com/user/Gangsline

https://twitter.com/Gangsline

JACOB
WHITTINGHAM

Jacob Whittingham has worked as the Programme Director for the award winning youth-led charity, SE1 United since 2003 in which he has developed several innovative youth projects providing mentoring and individual advocacy, conflict resolution, and promoting personal achievement. He has a BA (hons) in Philosophy, an MSc in International Politics, a

PGC in Youth and Community Work, and a PhD in Social Sciences researching mixed-race identity. He is also the author of the published book, 'What Being Black Is And What Being Black Isn't', an investigation into the stereotypes that are associated with young Black people in the UK. He has previously worked for the United Nations setting up youth projects in Eastern Europe, and has just finished working for the think-tank Race On The Agenda helping to improve teaching methods in schools working with young black males.

CLEON
WILSON

Cleon currently works as the Head of Behaviour and Mentoring at the outstanding City Academy, Hackney. Cleon also runs his own Training & Development Company specialising in School Governor training. Cleon Wilson through In Perspective Ltd strives to Empower - Train - Mentor - Coach and ultimately develop all kinds of people from any age or stage! Through programmes to support teachers and pastoral leaders to programmes to re-motivate disengaged at risk students, In Perspective Ltd perpetually strives to enrich both leaders and learners by any means and methods necessary!! It is clear to see that Cleon is a people person and has a passion for helping others to release their potential.

Most importantly Cleon is a Christian man after God's own heart, who is blessed to be father of one and a husband (the Author of this book!) 11 years strong!

AS BT ONCE SAID 'IT'S GOOD TO TALK':

@CleonWilson

@InPerspectiveUK

facebook.com/inperspectiveltd.com

linkedin.com/in/perspectiveltd

EJIKE
WODU

Ejike was raised in North London and is one of seven children. He has a MSc in Business Information Technology.

He is well traveled with experience of other cultures which he always embraces. Ejike is a lover of humankind and endeavours to see the best in individuals. He has represented Team GB in track and field and grew a wine retail business from scratch. Ejike always attempts to try things that are not usual.

He currently working as a Business Analyst/ Project Manager and is married with two children aged 11 and 7.

ABOUT 9:10 PUBLISHING

9:10 Publishing is a UK-based independent publishing company which was set up in 2012 with one aim in mind: to share our passion for the written word.

We believe that everyone should have the opportunity to read books that entertain, inform and enlighten. We publish a range of books with a specific focus on youth, business and community.

COMING TO A BOOK SHELF NEAR YOU IN SPRING 2016

MORE . . . LETTERS TO A YOUNG GENERATION

LETTERS TO A YOUNG GENERATION OF GIRLS